I'm not a copywriter, but ...

LESSONS LEARNED FROM A LATE BLOOMER

I'm not a copywriter, but ...

LESSONS LEARNED FROM A LATE BLOOMER

Joshua Womack

ISBN: 978-1-950843-55-8

Parafine Press
5322 Fleet Avenue
Cleveland, Ohio 44105
www.parafinepress.com
Cover design by Agape Creative
Book design by Meredith Pangrace

CONTENTS

PART II: THE WRITING

Foreword

What do stand-up comedy, professional wrestling, and chicken scratches have to do with copywriting?

In 2015, I was writing non-stop providing copy for a bevy of in-house clients. I was so busy that I didn't have time for a quick lunch, a long pee, or a brisk walk around our tidy Northeast Ohio campus.

One particular day, five more projects popped up in my already-exploding inbox. Pangs of panic struck my quivering body.

"I can't take it anymore!" I screamed at my boss. "I need some help. Anyone. I don't care! I need a copywriter."

"Relax," said my boss. "We'll get you some help."

After sifting through more than 300 good, bad, and just plain awful resumes, we finalized our list to three copywriter candidates.

I was about to email HR with the finalized candidates, when a designer walked up behind me and slid another resume onto my desk. The name at the top was Josh Womack.

This person gave me a smile, then a thumbs up, and said, "This is a good one. Trust me."

"He doesn't have any copywriting experience, though," I said, shaking my head.

"Did you have any copywriting experience when you started out?" the designer asked. "Just give him a chance. He's pretty funny."

"Funny how?" I asked, not trying to mimic the famous Joe Pesci scene from *Goodfellas*. "Like a circus clown funny?"

"No, he's a comedian."

My ears perked up.

"A comedian, eh?" I said.

I like comedians. I like funny people. Funny people are creative because they can think up jokes. Plus, funny people have the boldness to walk up on an empty stage and try to make a group of strangers laugh. It's hard. Trust me. I tried it. And I sucked.

"Okay," I said. "Let's see what this guy's got!"

And that's when I met Josh.

We were seated in a gray, unassuming, corporate interview room with fluorescent lights beaming upon our heads. I'd prepared for the interview with a handful of targeted selection questions supplied to me by HR—questions designed to separate the riff raff from the rubes.

He mentioned his stand-up career, which we talked extensively about. Then, he brought up professional wrestling.

"You were a professional wrestler?"

"Well, I signed up for a couple classes and thought it would be fun," he said.

I won't ruin Josh's story (which is in this novella) but it was pretty damn interesting.

Then came the portfolio review.

I'll be honest, there wasn't too much to review from his past jobs. Not a lot of copywriting work. Not a lot of marketing know-how. Not a lot of advertising acumen. I looked at the clock on the wall. Our hour was almost coming to an end.

"Wait a minute, I have something else," Josh said as he pulled out a couple sheets of paper from a folder. On it were a handful of chicken scratches and scribbles. I can't remember the context, but what I do remember were clever headlines, marketing-ish thoughts, and sparks of creativity—things that showed me he could do this job.

He had potential.

Then, like Anton Ego, the evil critic from the Pixar film *Ratatouille* after he bit into the French dish of stewed vegetables, I was thrown back to my first copywriting interview. No experience. No copywriting portfolio. No right being there.

But during that meeting, I had also pulled out my very own sketchbook of chicken scratches filled with ideas and sparks—the exact same thing that Josh did.

So, what do stand-up comedy, professional wrestling, and chicken scratches have to do with copywriting?

Well, just about anybody can be trained to write the right way. But the things you can't teach are the funny (stand-up), the fearlessness (wrestling), and the perseverance (chicken scratches). And that's why we decided to hire Josh.

Fast forward to a couple months after Mr. Womack's hire. Half of our creative team was in a big marketing brainstorm. We were all staring at a whiteboard, dry erase markers in our hands, trying to think up an awesome tagline for our Super Bowl Bingo Game. Viewers would punch their virtual bingo card when they came across a cliché commercial spot such as an explosion, a horse, or a cute baby. It was a good idea, but it needed an extra copywriting kick.

Lots of folks (including myself) were tossing out churlish quips, inane quotes, and putrid puns. Pretty much everything written on the whiteboard sucked.

Then, after a brief take, Josh Womack—the wrestler, the comedian, the overachiever—stood up and screamed, *"Your Game for the Big Game!"*

"Goddamn," I said to myself. "This guy's got it."

—Bradley Eimer
Associate Creative Director
Author of *Be The Dumbest Person In the Room*
And Other Life Lessons from a
Mid-Level Creative Schlub
Cleveland, Ohio
April 2022

Introduction

Something interesting happens when copywriters present their work. A lot of "copywriters" suddenly pop up.

Most of us have seen this happen at least once, maybe even a thousand times in our careers. You present your work to the account executive, client, or both. You and the designer take them through your thought process, why you went with the headlines you did, and the reasoning behind your precious words.

After some uncomfortable pauses, head tilts, and furrowed brows, the account executive breaks the silence with, "How about we go with [INSERT HEADLINE THEY CAME UP WITH ON THE SPOT]? Just a thought. I'm not a copywriter."

And then the floodgates open.

The client takes the account executive's cue and chimes in with, "I just think it could be stronger. I'm not a copywriter, but ..."

Wash, rinse, and repeat.

It's human nature to gravitate toward our own ideas, especially with something subjective like advertising.

And 99.9% of the time, the account executive or client means no ill will, they're just giving their two cents. Hence the title of this book.

As for the late bloomer part, I've always been a couple years behind the curve of "traditional" adulthood.

I didn't experience dorm life until I was 21. (The fact I don't drink kind of kills the fun part of this equation.)

I didn't get my undergraduate degree until I was 24. (Now, I didn't go to college until I was 19, so it wasn't exactly a *Tommy Boy* scenario.)

I didn't live on my own until I was 26.

I didn't get married until I was 37.

And to back up a few years, I didn't know what a copywriter was until I was 31. In a lot of ways, I still don't ... and if you look at the first couple years of my performance evaluations, a lot of my colleagues didn't think I was a copywriter either.

Who is this book for? "This is for the questions that don't have any answers, the midnight glancers ..." just kidding. And bonus points if you got the reference.

I picture this book in the hands of two types of people: junior copywriters facing some early-career obstacles and mid-level to senior copywriters looking for a quick burst of levity and inspiration.

If you're a junior copywriter who just got a less-than stellar performance review, like I did many times early in my career, this book is for you.

If you're a mid-level to senior copywriter who feels a bit stale and needs a reminder of how awesome being a copywriter is, this book is for you.

I'm still figuring things out. I'm sure you are, too. Hopefully you'll see some of yourself in the lessons I learned along the way.

I've included four short stories that influenced me as a person and as a copywriter. These aren't success stories by any means, but they are stories that impact my day-to-day writing. Everyone comes to copywriting with a past. This just happens to be mine.

Stand-up

A backhanded compliment can change your life. Like I said, I didn't know copywriting was a paying profession until I was 31, but in the years beforehand, I was getting creative experience. Just in a different field.

Thomas Kemeny, in his I-wish-I-would-have-written-that-book *Junior: Writing Your Way Ahead in Advertising*, talks about pre-copywriting experience and how valuable it is:

"Everyone has some past knowledge or history that they bring to the table. Past jobs or hobbies that define you. Put that into your work and it won't feel like an ad and won't look like anyone else's."

At the beginning of 2007, I started an internship with The Greater Cleveland Sports Commission. The internship qualified as the last credits I needed to get my degree in Sports Information from Bowling Green State University. A degree in Sports Management was all the rage in those days. Everyone thought they were somehow going to be the next *Jerry Maguire*. In reality, most of us started out in entry-level ticket sales for a minor league baseball or hockey team. When we finally figured out the hours and low pay, we decided to pursue other options.

A couple months into the internship, the vice president came into the interns' office. The office was a crammed, glorified storage room with myself and two other interns. I can't remember how it came to be, but the vice president—a gruff woman—said to me: "You're not a great intern, but you're kind of funny. Have you ever thought about doing stand-up?"

I laughed it off and went about my day. But being curious as to how one actually does or learns stand-up, I did a little digging.

After a quick Google search, I found a stand-up comedy workshop class in Cleveland. It was taught by a guy named Dave Schwensen, who had been a former comedian himself but had made his mark as a booker at Improv comedy clubs around the country. Dave was sort of a stand-up whisperer; he knew the business inside and out. He built a nice career teaching stand-up along with showing organizations how to use humor in the workplace effectively.

The workshop Dave taught consisted of three in-person classes where we would do our sets on the Cleveland Improv stage, then get feedback from Dave and the others in the class. He also taught the business of comedy and how to put together our press kit or reel. Finally, we performed in a "graduation showcase" at the Cleveland Improv for our friends and family brave enough to attend. You really have to love someone to see them attempt stand-up for the first time.

At the workshop classes, we would all take turns going up on stage and rambling. We thought we were hilarious ... but doing stand-up is hard. And doing stand-up in front of eight to ten people is torture, especially when you're just starting out.

I wish I could reach back and tell you the jokes I tried out, but I'm guessing the filters in my brain did their job of blocking out painful memories because I can't remember any of it. I probably did some hacky, easy bit about the Browns. You know, stuff only Clevelanders would find funny.

Dave was an effective instructor, though. He did a great job of navigating what topics were universal enough to be understood by everyone (relationships, family, grocery stores, etc.), and what topics were too "inside baseball." Now that I think about it, one guy tried telling a bit and his punchline was centered around this intricate UFC-type move that only UFC fans would understand. It would've killed inside the octagon. And probably with Joe Rogan.

The goal of the class was to come up with a three-minute set—an eternity when you're just starting out.

The night of our graduation showcase, I was both nervous and excited. There was a certain "first-timer" adrenaline rush. Being in my mid-20s and not having a sense of how the real world operated was a blessing. It was the perfect time to try stuff out before I had to face the consequences of adulthood.

I think I went up second. Maybe it was the adrenaline, maybe it was blind faith, but I remember feeling pretty good when I walked off stage. I know I didn't kill, but I managed to knock out my three minutes.

Dave, being the shrewd comedy businessman that he was, hired a guy to tape all the sets. So the class could buy a VHS copy of their sets for $20 each. I did ... and held onto it for a long time. I think I just threw it out. Probably better for all parties involved.

The truth is, even though I had a few jokes to hang my hat on, I didn't write nearly enough to become a real, full-time stand-up comedian. Dave told us a story about how comedian Drew Carey would write one new joke a week, so he'd have 52 new jokes each year. That level of consistency wasn't something I was ready to commit to. I enjoyed the social aspect of it more. Each stand-up show is like a little party, and you're the host.

I had about 12-15 minutes of tight, solid stuff. Sometimes with crowd work I could stretch it to 20 minutes. But to be a working comedian who actually makes a living at it, you need at least 30 minutes of tried-and-tested material.

The biggest lesson I learned from stand-up was how to think creatively. Like an "Introduction to Creativity" if it was a college class. I started to pay more attention to everything: my past, where I was at in life, things my friends and family would say. I was on the lookout for how I could make sense—and fun—of the world around me. Most importantly, my creative antenna started to pick up signals.

I looked up some of my old jokes. Most of them were lowbrow humor not worth including here. But now when I write copy, I have the stand-up experience to draw from. It helps keep headlines fun. And I'm happy to report this story has a happy ending.

Ten years after I did Dave's class, I got a call from my dad.

"Hey Dad, whaddya up to?"

"I'm driving downtown actually," he said.

"Cool. What for?"

"I'm taking Dave's comedy workshop like you did! Always wanted to try it, so I figured, what the hell."

What a moment. Here was my dad, at age 64, giving it a go. Me, my two brothers, and a bunch of our friends went down to cheer him on. He went on second, like I did ten years earlier, and did great.

Maybe the late bloomer thing is hereditary.

PART I: THE MIND

The Good Goo

A while back, I talked to a guy who used to write monologue jokes for Conan O'Brien. Late night monologue writers are machines, combing through the daily news and writing anywhere from 20–40 jokes in a day—with almost all of those jokes being irrelevant the next day. The kicker? Maybe one or two jokes make it on air.

He brought up the phrase "the good goo," which is that time of day where your brain is firing on all cylinders.

Your "good goo" might be first thing in the morning, or it might be late at night. Either way, protect it. It's a finite space of energy, focus, and creativity.

Early in your career, especially if you write best in the morning, you might have to make compromises when people schedule early meetings. But the more established you get, the more you'll feel confident in declining those meetings to concentrate on why you were hired: to think, read, and write.

My sweet spot is first thing in the morning. There's a quote Steven Pressfield (who I'll reference more in this book) shared in his best seller, *The War of Art: Winning the Inner Creative Battles*, about writer W. Somerset Maugham.

Someone once asked the great author if he wrote on a schedule or only when inspiration struck him. "I write only when inspiration strikes me," Maugham replied. "Fortunately, it strikes me every morning at nine o'clock sharp."

Maugham respected "the good goo."

Nobody Writes All Day

In December of 2020, Jerry Seinfeld was a guest on the podcast, *The Tim Ferriss Show*. Seinfeld was talking about his daughter, who like him, has a creative gift but finds herself struggling to sit down to do the work.

Seinfeld's advice is straightforward: Schedule writing sessions. Put a half hour or hour on the calendar and do as much as you can. When the allotted time is up, walk away.

He explains:

> I told my daughter, "Just do an hour. That's a lot."
>
> She said, "I'm going to write all day."
>
> I said, "No, you're not. Nobody writes all day. Shakespeare can't write all day. It's torture."

You may disagree with this, remembering a time where you were working on a rush project and were forced to write for 8+ hours on a particular day.

But I tend to agree with him. There will be days when unexpected requests will come in and you'll need to knock out last-minute revisions. But for me, 90 minutes of deep work a day is more doable over the long haul. Your number might be 45 minutes, or it might be two to three hours. The amount of time doesn't matter. The amount of time that's right for you does.

Are You In A Good Place?

I used to be one of those people who enjoyed going into the office. Not necessarily for the social aspect because as soon as I would sit down, I'd start writing. It was more for the routine. I always left work at work, knowing any writing I did in the evening probably didn't have as much juice as my morning writing.

Just because I stopped writing at 5 p.m. didn't mean I stopped thinking. Like Andrew Boulton says in his book *Copywriting Is ... : 30-or-So Thoughts on Thinking Like a Copywriter*, "No matter what your timesheet tells you, there's no such thing as downtime in copywriting."

The daily commute, morning writing time, lunchtime workout, and afternoon meetings were fine by me, mostly because it was the only work setup I—and most of us—had ever known. It was the office, and that's where everyone worked.

When COVID hit, I was terrified my routine would be thrown all out of whack. I was such a fan of routine that I continued to go into the office for two weeks after everyone went home. Finally, my boss said I had to stay home.

My wife, sensing my uneasiness, knew that if I could get into a routine writing at home, I'd be fine. She went out and found a small desk, brought it home, and put it together. (My wife is much more patient at putting things together than me. I like to think I contributed by taking the dog out for a few hours so she could assemble in peace.)

Once I had my work space in the corner of our spare room, I was set. I had a space—and quickly, a routine.

Since working remotely, I've done my best writing. In my opinion, the best thing COVID did for copywriters was eliminate the distractions of the office.

Distractions like:

- Unnecessary standing meetings first thing in the morning when you could be writing
- The assumption that if you're not at your desk after 4 p.m. then you're not a hard worker
- Office celebrations that you feel obligated to attend

Most copywriters just want to be left alone. Of course, there are brainstorming meetings and presentations that are part of the job. But for the copywriters that I've known, an hour to themselves is worth its weight in gold. Working remotely provides less office politics and optics and more of that "good goo."

With that said, I understand not every copywriter wants to work from home. I confess there is a certain psychological safety that one feels with people nearby. And the delightful surprise when a free lunch would pop up every now and then.

Your habits are unlike anyone else's. I work with a fellow writer who starts every morning sipping on hot water. Not coffee, tea, or hot chocolate, just *hot water*. Whatever warms up your mind, I guess.

If you miss the office dynamic, try working at a coffee shop or a co-working space. As a copywriter, it's probably in your nature to test things out. The important part is to find the right space that works for you.

Keep Slingin'

About three years into my career came a tipping point. My boss told me I wasn't "getting it" and that some of my colleagues felt the same way. There was a perception that I wasn't invested in the work. For one project in particular, my boss said they would have to bring in another writer if I didn't shape up.

Now, I wish I could've told you that I was a wet-behind-the-ears, straight-out-of-college graduate simply learning hard lessons. I was learning lessons, but I wasn't exactly a young pup. I was 35.

The words stung and my pride took a hit. But the biggest blow came to my confidence. With all the negative feedback, I started to write scared, like a pitcher afraid to throw a fastball.

Instead of using the experience and skills that landed me the job in the first place, I started to walk on eggshells with every headline. I was afraid to take chances, so I didn't play to win. I just played not to lose.

It took eight to ten months for my confidence to slowly come back. And it was right about a year after that incident when I finally felt comfortable slingin' crazy ideas again.

If you ever find yourself in the position I was in, keep slingin'. Obviously, you want to pay attention to the brief and what the customer wants, but don't let fear get in the way of having a good time writing your copy. Keep having fun; it'll come through in your writing.

Feedback:
It's Part of the Game

I think one of the reasons I struggled with feedback early in my career is because I didn't understand it. It felt too personal. I viewed it as an attack on my character and my writing. I also didn't fully understand that most times, copywriters don't get things right on the first try.

My thinking changed when I talked to a career coach who explained a more positive way to look at feedback. She said:

> *"Think of a basketball game. There are the fans, the people selling hot dogs and beer, the coaches, the refs, the players on the bench. Then there's you, playing in the game. You're where most copywriters want to be ... "*

(My first thought was: I'd like to be employed.)

> *"... in the game."*

This analogy goes to show you that just trying is the most important thing you can do. Much like basketball players, getting onto the court is the first step.

Another similar piece of advice came from Brad Stulberg, co-author of the *The Passion Paradox: A Guide to Going All In, Finding Success, and Discovering the Benefits of an Unbalanced Life.*

"All kinds of people have all kinds of opinions; if you try to write for everyone, you'll end up writing for no one. People not loving your stuff is part and parcel of the gig, it's going to happen if you have skin in the game."

Luckily, I grew out of taking everyone else's opinions to heart. And even more lucky, I'm still in the game. If you're struggling with this as well, try to remember that not everyone is going to like your work, but continuing to show up and do your job is 90% of what being a copywriter is.

Don't Be
That Copywriter

A talented copywriter can write just about everything: email, direct mail, scripts, social, etc.

A talented but arrogant copywriter can write just about everything: email, direct mail, scripts, social, etc.

The difference between the two? The first copywriter knows they're not the only writer in the world, or at the agency.

A talented copywriter can be confident, but in the same breath be unsure and vulnerable.

Don't be the second copywriter. Believe in your ideas, but don't believe you're the only one with ideas.

Don't Fear the Reaper (AKA the Eyeballs)

Early on, I got very nervous when my writing was presented to small groups. I called one of the monthly meetings, "the firing range." Basically, everyone in the meeting, like project managers and creative management, were paid to poke holes in my stuff.

In any artistic field, you're confessing to the reader or client how you interpret the world through your words. Yeah, you're writing for them, but a little part of you always comes through.

Over time, you won't fear the eyeballs on your work anymore, you'll embrace them. You did the hard part: the writing. Critiquing is the easy part. Your confidence will pick up the more you present. Most project managers and clients wish they could do what you do. It's a healthy reminder you're at the table for a reason.

... But Stay (A Little) Scared

Even though I just told you to have confidence when presenting your work, here I am telling you to stay a little scared. What gives?

The sweet spot is right in the middle, or having a healthy fear.

I still get a little scared over anything I have to write. Usually, the feeling sets in the night before when I think about reading through the brief the next morning. Will I understand the objective? What if I have to ask the project manager a dumb question for clarity?

The next morning as I'm coming out of the shower, it's still on my mind. But once I sit down and knock out that first headline, the fear begins to evaporate. I'm always grateful for this healthy fear, though. It lets me know that I'm still being challenged on a consistent basis, and that little bit of fear when I'm writing helps to fuel my creativity.

Amateur or Pro?

Adversity will rear its ugly head at different points in your career. This happened to me when I saw every other copywriter at my job get promoted before me—and they all started after me.

Now, most of them came into the agency with a lot more experience, so it really wasn't anything I could control, but my shortsightedness and bruised ego couldn't see the forest for the trees. I guess it was a volatile cocktail of immaturity and lack of experience.

The more I reflect on this time, the more I think about author Steven Pressfield's whole idea of life as an amateur vs. life as a pro. At this time in my career, I was definitely an amateur, and this passage from Pressfield's *Turning Pro: Tap Your Inner Power and Create Your Life's Work* sums up where my head was at:

"The amateur is a narcissist. He views the world hierarchically. He continuously rates himself in relation to others, becoming self-inflated if his fortunes rise, and desperately anxious if his star should fall."

We've all been passed over for a promotion. And it's hard not to have all the feelings that go with it, like resentment and jealousy.

Nowadays, I give myself 24–48 hours to be disappointed, sad, or pissed off when something doesn't go my way. For you, it might be shorter or a bit longer.

As tough as it is, suck up your pride, congratulate those who got promoted instead of you, and quietly go back to writing. Your time will come.

Abandoned Buildings Are Good for the Brain

Now, the idea of walking outside to gain clarity isn't something new. But it was new to me.

In February of 2020, my wife and I got a dog. The next month, COVID hit, and I started working from home. Naturally, I started walking more because of the dog.

I was never much of a walker just for walking's sake. When I was still going into the office, I used to judge all the people who would walk around our work campus. My thought was, "We have a gym here; why don't you just go there? Do you *really* want to be known as a mall walker?" (In this case, it was a work campus walker, but you get the point.)

But now I get it. Walking is sustainable, and it's something you don't need a ton of discipline to do. And for me, walking by abandoned buildings with my dog is a daily habit that keeps my brain thinking up new possibilities.

I live in a downtown area. Whenever I start to feel stuck or impatient from sitting at the computer, I leash up my dog and we head out.

One of the unforeseen benefits of being in an urban area, especially post-COVID, is seeing all the commercial real estate available. Some of the buildings are recently vacated while some have been empty for a while.

Whenever I walk by one of these buildings, I think to myself, "A cool, tech startup would be great in this space." Or "I could picture myself living in an apartment here." Or "I wonder what occupied this space in the 80s, 90s, or early 2000s."

Walking is creative cardio. It gets your imagination pumping.

... So Is Shaking the Etch A Sketch

Remember the Etch A Sketch? The red frame with the gray screen is a staple of most 90s childhoods. You'd turn the little white knobs and create whatever came to your imagination. After you grew tired or ashamed of what you created, you'd simply pick up the toy, shake it over your head, and start with a clean screen.

For about seven years now, I've been using the sauna as my mental Etch A Sketch. Some time between 11 a.m. and 1 p.m., I try to get in 15–25 minutes of sauna time in addition to a little cardio. When I was still going into the office, I was lucky enough to work somewhere that had a nice gym and sauna in the building. It quickly became my refuge: a place to warm my mind and soul.

I can't stress enough how important this downtime is. After a morning of writing, reading briefs, and perhaps a meeting or two, the sauna acts as a midday break, or an oil change for my brain. Sweating out the morning's stress helps me reset for a productive afternoon. It's my version of shaking the Etch A Sketch.

The sauna for me is a log cabin vacation I get to take every day. This works for me; meditation or something else may work for you. The important part is to enjoy the "not writing" part of your day as much as the time when you're writing.

The Book is the Buffalo

Native Americans hunted buffalo not just for food but to sustain their way of life. The skin was used for tipis; fur for robes; and bones and horns for digging sticks and spoons. Copywriters use books in the same way.

Here are a few ways I optimize books and everything they have to offer.

Read the book and highlight favorite passages. Write down highlighted parts in a Word doc and save to the computer (obviously a physical notebook works too).

Write a blog or book report on what you've learned. This is a great way to summarize everything you learned and refer back to it when needed.

Email the author and tell them what you learned. Since authors and copywriters are birds of the same feather, I'm guessing words of affirmation are our primary love languages. Tell the author what you learned and what you loved.

Lend the book to a friend. Then when you get the book back, read it again.

We just don't read books to learn, we read for the survival of our most important hunting tool: our minds.

Connecting
People and Ideas

More realizations that didn't happen until I was almost 40:

If you can connect ideas, you'll be a good writer.

If you can connect people, you'll be a good networker.

If you can connect people and ideas, you'll be in another stratosphere.

Good ideas can only go so far in our copywriter brains. Even though many of us would rather spend an hour with a Word doc rather than with a living, breathing person, eventually we're going to need people to help carry out our visions.

Getting excited about other people's ideas is the first step. This is especially true in the work-from-home world we live in now. No longer are many of us in a room all together throwing ideas onto a white board. In the pre-COVID world, you could read people's body language and see if they were feeling an idea. You could see them, smile, and nod. Now, many of us prefer not to turn on our cameras.

One thing I've been trying to get better at is vocalizing or typing my enthusiasm into the Teams chat when a good idea pops up from my peers. Sometimes I repeat the praise because it's easy to feel like you're in a Zoom or Teams abyss.

This over-communication soft skill took me a few years to develop. This isn't to say you need to email or message every thought you have. That's what Facebook is for. It's simply updating your co-workers in a professional, consistent way.

In an agency or in-house setting, it's more of staying on the same page with your fellow copywriters, art directors, and creative directors. I have a rule that if I know I'll be away from my computer for more than two hours, I'll shoot a quick message to my team.

This works for brainstorming and working on projects, too. Sometimes I'll just shoot over a few headlines to the art director I am working with. I'll let them know the body copy is still percolating but that the headlines should at least give them an idea of the visuals. This isn't life-changing advice by any means, but it's the day-to-day social WD-40 that keeps work relationships moving.

Ed Catmull describes this kind of thought process in his book, *Creativity, Inc.: Overcoming the Unseen Forces That Stand in the Way of True Inspiration.*

"Don't wait for things to be perfect before you share them with others. Show early and show often."

About a year and a half ago I was part of a small team that had to come up with a direct mail kit. At the time, *The Queen's Gambit* was all the rage on Netflix, so we decided to do a chess-themed concept for the mailing.

We weren't quite sure how it was going to look, but I figured a few amusing lines might help the designers get started. The mailing was for a home insurance offer.

Be the grandmaster of great protection
Say "checkmate" to high rates!
Don't be a pawn to high rates
Protect your new castle
A winning strategy for your home
Home insurance that's three steps ahead

I didn't have the body copy ready, and the lines weren't perfect, but they were worth sharing to help build creative momentum.

A Final Thought on the Ego

Here's a short example of why copywriters and comedians aren't that different.

Let's say you're the copywriter on a radio spot and you've written a 60-second script. After feedback, legal, and PR take a look, the script that makes it to air has exactly 20 seconds of stuff you wrote.

It's a killer spot. It wins awards. The client and your creative director are happy. But you're fuming. You had so much more to say!

A similar situation happened to me when I did stand-up.

Many times I would be emceeing at a comedy club and the booker told me I'd do 15 minutes up front. Great! I had my tried-and-true stuff for 12 minutes, and along the way, I figured I'd pepper in a couple new bits I was pretty sure would work.

Fifteen minutes before the show, the booker would say the headliner wanted to do 70 minutes instead of 60 minutes, so those 10 minutes were taken off my stage time.

What started at 15 minutes was now down to 5 minutes. How could they?!

This sort of thing happened to me all the time. I would get upset over something that was out of my control, and in turn, would get onstage in a bad headspace. I'd be so frustrated about the 10 minutes that were taken away that I forgot to put the energy into the 5 minutes I still had.

Not until I stopped doing stand-up did I realize the audience didn't care how long I was on stage—only I did. They just cared if I made them laugh, not how old I was or how much time was shaved off my set. It was a lesson I wish I would've learned in real time.

In our business, sometimes all the client or creative director wants is a line. It might not even be a clever or comical line, just a line that gets the job done. All those great lines they passed on? Well, save them for a rainy day. There will be something new to write tomorrow, and you never know when you could use the lines you came up with or adaptations of them. Don't let your ego now stand in the way of finishing a project.

P.S. Ironically, the "stage time" mindset crept its way into writing this book. But instead of minutes on stage, it was word count. I kept beating myself up thinking if I didn't write at least 10,000 words then I didn't deserve to write a book. I guess old insecurities die hard.

LAUGH STAFF

In the thick of my mildly successful, part-time stand-up career, I was introduced to someone who would change the course of my writing life.

I met Cameron through my friend, Steve. Steve and I went to high school together and even roomed together for a year in college. At the time I was doing stand-up, Steve was pursuing his MBA at Cleveland State. One of his classmates, Cameron, was interested in learning a little bit about stand-up, so he reached out to me to ask if I'd look over his jokes.

I went to Cameron's condo and read what he had. I remember thinking that for his first time writing jokes, this guy was pretty good. I also remember the only thing he had in his fridge were two Red Bulls, which explained his enthusiastic, all-over-the-place-nature.

I went to support Cameron at his first open mic, and he did well. He came to a couple of my shows and we kept in touch.

A couple months after we met, he called me with a funny story.

Cameron was at a wedding for one of his friends.

The groom approached him with an interesting request before the reception started.

"Hey Cam, listen, I know my best man is going to make an ass out of himself when he gives his speech. I know you've been doing some stand-up so can I ask a favor? When he's done with his toast, can you stand up and say a few words after? I don't want the room to be in a bad place and figured you might be able to get a few laughs."

Being the mensch that he is, Cameron agreed to help out. Sure enough, the best man rambled on about god knows what. After, Cameron stood up with a few "impromptu" remarks and got some laughs. The evening proceeded.

Later on during the reception, another one of the groomsmen approached Cameron.

"Hey, saw what you did up there and loved it! I am going to be the best man in another wedding a couple months from now. Would you help me write my speech with a few jokes? I'll pay you."

Enter Laugh Staff.

Cameron asked me, in not so many words, "What if we start a company where stand-up comedians write wedding toasts?"

I was intrigued. And I liked the fact that Cameron presented it as a way for comedians to make money during the day while they paid their dues hitting the stages at night.

Cameron and I were full steam ahead. No, really, Cameron's full-time job was that of tugboat captain! A tugboat captain with an MBA starting a comedic speech writing business. Maybe he should be writing this book.

Cameron's enthusiasm was palpable, and he had an entrepreneurial spirit that really got us off the ground. He got a couple of friends to invest in the company and started working on a business plan. He also took it upon himself to work with a web design company to build out an e-commerce site.

My job was to round up comedians. I reached out to a few comics I had worked with and then asked a few other comedians for individuals they thought would enjoy this type of work. Our initial team consisted of ten or so comedians. The two biggest names we had were Jay Black and Curtis Cook.

I had worked with Jay at Hilarities in Cleveland. He was a former high school English teacher who made the jump to stand-up and never looked back. (In my experience, former teachers always made awesome

I'm not a copywriter, but ...

stand-up comedians, since they had a captive audience: the classroom.) Jay opened frequently for guys like Brad Garretty and Kevin Nealon.

As for Curtis, he and I had done some shows together around town. He was young, having just graduated from The College of Wooster, but like Jay, was receptive to the idea of Laugh Staff. He was also responsive and respectful, which were rarities for comedians. Eventually, he went on to be a writer for Comedy Central's *The Jim Jeffries Show* and wrote for HBO Max's *Friends: The Reunion*.

Before I go any further, I should probably tell you how we settled on the name Laugh Staff. Cameron had started thinking of some names, and he had a web/marketing company think of names too. I found an old email from 2013 when we were in the naming process. Here it is:

Josh,
We need to decide on a name so I can start the formation of the company and have the logo designed to put into the business plan. Here are a few I came up with:
- TrueAmigo
- Laughline
- Speechologist

- Speechon
- Laughwrites
- Confidencecrew
- Cheersfriends
- Cheers to the night
- Speech Hero
- Speechman (kind of play off the super hero theme ... like superman and spiderman)
- Speech and Teach
- Storytellers
- Raise your glass
- Speechpants (like don't get caught without your pants, or speech)

Here are some the marketing group came up with... nothing seems to excite me so far.

- www.speechomony.com
- www.speechsmith.com
- www.insertlaughter.com
- www.speechguru.com
- www.speechly.com
- www.speechbutler.com

Talk soon,

Cameron

Looking back, it probably would've helped a ton if we'd actually had "speech" somewhere in the title (to help with SEO/people actually finding us online). But Laugh Staff conveyed two things we were after: the comedy element and the company element. At the time, we thought "staff" made us sound legit.

From a creative standpoint, Laugh Staff provided me with my unofficial introduction to creative briefs. Every time somebody bought a speech package (there were three speech packages available), an automated questionnaire would be sent to the customer asking for relevant speech information.

In the questionnaire, we'd ask for basic info like:

- Groom/Bride Name
- Age
- Occupation
- Interests/Hobbies
- Siblings' Names and Ages
- Parents' Names
- Parents' Marital Status
- Number of Wedding Guests
- Percentage of People You Know at the Wedding

Then we'd go a little deeper with questions like:

- Why did the bride/groom choose you to be the maid of honor/best man?
- How did the bride and groom meet?
- What's something you love about the bride/groom?
- Describe the first time you met the bride/groom.
- Tell us about the engagement.
- Can you pull off sarcastic jokes?
- Are you nervous about this speech?
- Do you have an accent or any unique physical characteristics?

The majority of the time, I never actually talked with the customers; I can remember maybe two or three phone calls. But I think this is how we (the customer and myself) preferred it. It was just email, the preferred communication method of Millennials worldwide, next to texting.

The answers they provided gave me a peek into their personalities. How the customer answered the questions revealed how much they were willing to push the envelope. If someone included some f-bombs and inappropriate stories in their answers, I knew I could straddle the line of a PG-13 or R-rated speech. If the answers were more concise and hinted at a religious or conservative personality, I knew to keep things PG.

My curiosity into these people's lives helped make Laugh Staff more human. If I got a questionnaire back that was bare bones, I'd email the customer directly, putting a real person behind this crazy, little-known company they've entrusted to capture their words.

My emails always went something like this:

Hi Mandy,

Josh here. I'm pumped to write your speech; sounds like you and Vanessa are pretty close. I wanted to see if I could dig just a little deeper with a few more questions.
Growing up, was there any celebrity Vanessa had a crush on that she dreamed of marrying?
Did you and Vanessa ever go through any bad fashion phases?
When did you know Todd was different?

Thanks,
Josh

Taking an interest in the speech givers was almost as important as the speech content itself. Why? Because we were asking people to talk about their favorite subject: themselves.

I tried to dig deep into the younger/adolescent years of the best man or maid of honor. Nostalgia, I thought, was a good way to get the maid of honor or best man comfortable telling stories. It also went over well with crowds, as most of us can smile as we look back on what we thought was cool or trendy.

Like I said, the majority of these speech exchanges were through email. My goal with every speech was to have the customer at least smile or smirk a couple times when they first read it. (If they snorted, even better.)

Here is an excerpt of a maid of honor speech where, based on how she answered the questionnaire, I knew I could push things a little:

> *Good evening everyone! For those I haven't met, my name is Ellie and I am honored to be standing next to Jess as her maid of honor.*
>
> *Jess, I can't begin to tell you how beautiful you look today. You're elegant, timeless, and a reflection of perfection. And in a total girl-crush type of way, you're smokin' hot.*

I'm the maid of honor so I'm allowed to say that. Seriously Daniel, you got yourself a dime right here! Jess has the hips, lips, and fingertips to make an honest man out of you.

As you can see, the maid of honor was comfortable in her abilities and didn't mind being a bit brash with her words. Remember how I said every copywriter comes to the table with their own, unique past? "Hips, lips, and fingertips" is something a buddy of mine used to say in middle school about girls he wanted to go out with. Always stuck with me. Can you think of any fun, memorable lines your friends said growing up? If so, jot them down. They might just find a place in a future headline or body copy.

Some of you already know the story of how Jess and Daniel met, but some of you may not. Daniel's boss got his hair cut by Jess and told Daniel about this pretty Maltese girl who cuts hair and that Daniel just had to meet her.

Daniel wasted no time and, in chronological order, did the following. As you can tell by the series of events, the creepiness factor escalates quickly.

Added Jess on Facebook ... OK, no big deal.

Started Direct Messaging her ... Pretty weird, but still not too bad.

Showed up for a haircut with no appointment scheduled ... we call this "Stalker Level 1"

Waited a few days and then sent her flowers at work ... and at this point it was a full-on Stage 5 Clinger/Stalker Level 3

With wedding speeches, attention spans can be tough. Most people just want to get to dancing and free drinks. Numbering a series of events can slow the speech down so the audience can follow along. This also works when writing emails or direct mail when listing the benefits of the product.

When Jess told me all of this, I told her to burn his number immediately! But, Jess did the exact opposite and got herself a great guy who she can't picture life without.

Daniel has been great for Jess. He works tirelessly to make sure they have a good life and handles her feisty personality well. Most of you know Daniel is an accomplished "Tradie" and though he works well with his hands, he works even better with his heart.

Daniel builds beautiful things everyday and now he has the most beautiful girl to call his wife.

Jess, you've been like a sister to me, and my life, along with everybody that knows you, is better because of your spirit and kindness. I know you and Daniel will have a great future together.

If we can all raise our glasses.

Jess and Daniel, like most great love stories of our generation, Facebook brought you together. But your love and respect for one another has kept you together. Make today the day that you love each other the least. And make the most of every day tomorrow and forever. Love you guys; cheers!

Obviously, nobody is going to confuse the above with The Gettysburg Address. Some of the lines might even seem corny. But for the person reading it, they could roll with it or just take out parts that they didn't feel were "them." Sometimes it's better to give too much rather than not enough, and you can use that same approach in copywriting.

Below is a maid of honor example that skews a little more heartfelt:

> *Hi everyone! My name is Anna, and I just wanted to take a couple moments to say a few words about Rebecca, Aaron, and how great they are together.*
>
> *Rebecca is that rare type of friend who finds new ways to surprise and inspire you. When she asked me to be her maid of honor, she wrote me a letter.*

A letter is so personal. You can imagine someone unfolding it, and stopping to read it, and maybe reading it again. It also gets the audience wanting to know what was in the letter. And it sounds better than, "When she asked me to be her maid of honor, she sent me a text." You can use this personalized approach in your copywriting as well. What's going to make your end user feel special?

The letter she wrote reflected many of the qualities I love about her. Those qualities being sincerity and imaginative thinking mixed in with a sense of warmth you only get from the rarest of friends.

Rebecca has a way of elevating every moment. It could be a simple conversation you're having with her at a coffee shop, or the way she interacts with her patients at work.

She gives each interaction the two things we all crave most: attention and care. She has an effortlessly authentic way of connecting with others.

When she met Aaron, those attributes were only amplified. They say your best friend brings out the best in you. Aaron pushes Rebecca to be her best. He's always there with a kind word or a warm smile, or sometimes, when words aren't necessary, he's simply there to listen and love.

In her questionnaire, the maid of honor did an awesome job of conveying the simplicity of the relationship between the bride and groom, much like you should keep things simple within your headlines and body copy. For them, there weren't any extravagant proposals or near-death experiences, just an appreciation for the day-to-day interactions. "Elevating every moment/When words aren't necessary."

Rebecca, I know as long as you have Aaron and a bag of Hot Cheetos by your side, you'll be well taken care of. The two of you complement each other beautifully. You've been thousands of miles away with nothing but a backpack and found the beauty in every moment. Today, you have your friends and family all in one place, for you, with nothing but love.

I wish you guys success on many more adventures, including this awesome one called marriage. Cheers!

In this final part, she was able to inject a little personality despite this speech being a more sincere one. Even when you're writing more serious copy, make sure you don't make it stuffy.

In the span of seven years, I wrote about 200 speeches. Stand-up introduced me to creative writing, and Laugh Staff helped me tell stories with structure. Cameron and I believed that a best man or maid of honor speech might be the closest opportunity one has to stand-up in their lifetime (if they decided to go the humorous route). Therefore, we wanted to write the best "set" or speech we could.

Maybe the toast gave the best man the confidence to dance with the bride's cousin. And maybe they went out on a date. And maybe they got married and started a family. Who knows?!

Needless to say, Laugh Staff was exciting and experimental. And it was the biggest feather in my cap having not had agency or traditional copywriting experience.

Stephen King would scold me for using too many adverbs in my speeches, but for a best man or maid of honor, I could get away with it. No way I would still be a copywriter without Laugh Staff. So thanks, Cameron.

PART II:
THE WRITING

Headlines: The Safe, the Stretch, and the Really Far Out There

Write the safe headline first. This headline answers the brief, and most likely, the client will approve it.

Write the stretch headline next. This headline still speaks to the brief but gives a little smirk; it shows your creativity, or personality, peeking through.

Write the really far out there headline last. This headline probably won't get picked, but write it anyway. As copywriters, we're hired to come up with ideas. Give the world a glimpse into your twisted brain. This is the headline only YOU can come up with.

Another gem from Ed Catmull in *Creativity, Inc.: Overcoming the Unseen Forces That Stand in the Way of True Inspiration*:

"Always take a chance on better, even if it seems threatening."

Last year myself and a few other copywriters were tasked with coming up with a name for a car warranty offer. It was an amusing exercise, or at least as fun as car warranties can be.

We brainstormed the usual words like "vehicle," "protection," and "guard." But then we dug a little deeper. One of the words I played around with was "Phew", signifying the relief one would have knowing they have the warranty. I thought it could be written as:

Phew!
A car warranty from [COMPANY]

It was entertaining; different; and provided an inquisitive and positive spin on one of life's necessary evils, like car warranties. I thought it could play well in the social media and direct mail space too.

We ended up sending ten names to the customer. And I'm sad to report, "Phew!" came in last place.

The moral of the story is: We as a creative team tried to take a chance on "better." Was it a failure? Not in the least. It made it into this book, didn't it? It also remains one of the more fun projects in recent memory.

A Copywriter's
Best Friends

Subject lines, preheaders, and headlines have helped me in more ways than I can count. If I'm feeling overwhelmed by a project or if I have to write multiple things in one day, I simply aim for a goal of knocking out the subject lines, preheaders, and headlines before lunch just to get something on paper. Most of the time, the momentum will carry me into writing the body copy too, at least finishing what Ann Handley rightfully calls "the ugly first draft."

If the project is a direct mail kit, I simply try to write the headlines that will go on the front or the back of the envelope. Again, the body copy will come soon enough.

About a year ago, I picked up a book by the Harvard Business Review called *Focus: Emotional Intelligence*. In the book, one of the authors, Monique Valcour, references a TED Talk from University of Minnesota professor Teresa Glomb.

Glomb talks about organizing your workday for a "downhill start" which consists of some easy tasks first thing in the morning to help you feel productive and confident as you start the day. (It's the same concept described in the bestselling book *Make Your Bed: Little Things That Can Change Your Life … And Maybe the World* by retired U.S. Navy Admiral William H. McRaven.)

When a day of writing feels insurmountable, lean on your best friends. Subject lines, preheaders, and headlines will be there for you.

Look At That Body (Copy)

For me, body copy rolls downhill after you write the headline. The headline gets your main point across, but the body copy gets you to believe in the product or service that you might purchase.

It's like seeing a brand new truck on the lot. You love how it looks—and how you'll look in it. Then the car salesperson tells you about the heated seats, Bluetooth capabilities, backup camera, etc. The car's features are the body copy: the stuff that reinforces the great decision you're about to make.

Three reasons to believe are a good rule of thumb when it comes to writing body copy, either for email or direct mail. If you're writing about lasik eye surgery, three obvious benefits might be:

Convenience Night and weekend appointments and procedures available
Cost Installment plans for cost of the procedure
Savings No more buying contact solutions or new prescriptions

If those are too basic, and you wanted to dig a little deeper, you could go more emotional, like:

No more f-ups! No more fog ups when you're wearing a mask and your lenses get steamy
Freedom to Roam Finally, you can go swimming and not worry about a contact lens falling out
Confidence, Man Maybe you felt like glasses were holding you back in the looks or dating department

Let's try one more. How about if you're writing for a financial planner?

Expertise & History Our financial planners have served over [#] clients since [year]
Budget-friendly Hiring a financial planner doesn't have to break the bank. In fact, we'll help you keep more in the bank. (I know this is hacky, but you get the point.)
Versatile We've helped large families, Baby Boomers, single people, etc. from all lines of work (business professionals, teachers, tradespeople, etc.).

Now let's try to dig just a bit more.

Exhale! Money management is a personal and scary thing for some. Now you can breathe easy knowing someone is looking out for you.

Wow, it's doable. Whether it's a nice retirement or your future dream home, your financial planner has laid out a clear plan to help you get what you've been dreaming of.

A Better You I feel like a better mother/father/ sibling/individual knowing that I am laying out a better future for myself, my loved ones, and the things I care about (charities, alma mater, etc.).

Obviously these are just a jumping off point, but hopefully you can see the cadence. I chose lasik and financial planning because they aren't the sexiest things to write about, but they're just as important.

Every product has a story. Even if it's boring, you can find the interesting nuggets of truth if you look deep enough.

The One(s) that Got Away

Chances are you're going to work with other talented copywriters. Every now and then, they'll write something you'll be envious of. In your mind, or out loud if you're comfortable in your own skin, you'll say, "I wish I would've written that."

This acknowledgment is good on many levels.

First, it shows your ego isn't so large as to deny the fact that other people can write just as well or better than you.

Second, it shows maybe, just maybe, if you would've spent a little more time on the task, you would've thought of the idea, too.

Third, it shows you've still got a lot to learn. Learning is key.

Try to find comfort in the fact that, inevitably, people have said the same thing about lines you've written.

Get to the Joke Quicker

One night, a fellow stand-up comedian gave me my first lesson in editing. He said:

"I really liked your stuff. Funny. I think you can get the audience laughing sooner though. Go back and see how many words it takes to get your first laugh. I bet you can shave off 20–30 words and get to the punchline quicker."

I went back to my Word doc and realized my first laugh came roughly 80 words in. I took some stuff out, shortened some sentences, and got it down to 55 words.

The next night, I tried my shortened intro, and wouldn't you know, the laugh came sooner.

About a year into my copywriting career, I met a brilliant writer who wrote so simply it was frustrating. Whatever I wrote in seven or eight words she could convey in four or five! Or three and a few emojis.

Eventually, from working with her on so many projects, I too began to write more clearly and concisely. It takes a lot of effort to write so simply.

Seek out people that push you to be more concise, and keep practicing at it. When an idea can be captured more quickly, it's easier for consumers to digest.

Direct Mail: Go for it!

For me, direct mail was where I learned the most about copywriting and how all the pieces fit together.

Direct mail doesn't quite sizzle like social media, TV, or radio, but it doesn't mean it's any less important. Clients love it primarily for two reasons: It's trackable and cheap. (Sorry, I meant cost-efficient, nothing we put out there is "cheap," right?)

If you're early in your career, jump at the chance to work on direct mail kits. Every agency needs at least one copywriter who can come up with a cohesive message for the front of the envelope, the back of the envelope, the letter itself, and the tear-away card (if the kit calls for one).

Being the go-to writer for direct mail will make you a favorite with your creative director and your clients.

A piece of advice I got early on was each headline on the front of the envelope, back of the envelope, and tear away card should be able to live on its own.

Picture a family's crowded kitchen table with a bunch of "junk" mail, or a small business owner with a cluttered desk of papers. Can someone look at the back of your envelope and decipher exactly "What's in it for me"?

If the person does decide to tear away the card and stuff it in their wallet, will they know exactly what you're offering when they pull out the card in the waiting room at the dentist's office?

A lot of veteran copywriters probably already know this, but for those junior copywriters just getting their feet wet, something to remember is Ed Mayer's "40-40-20" rule:

40% Audience
40% Offer
20% Design and Copy

As a new writer, you're probably still getting familiar with who the mailing is going to and what the nuts and bolts of the offer are (i.e. bundling and saving on insurance, cash back on credit cards, the possibility of saving over $XXX if you sign up now).

Once you know the audience and the offer, you can start on the design and copy. The more background you have, the better.

MONOLOGUE JOKES

About a year into copywriting, I became obsessed with monologue jokes. I wanted to know who wrote them and, more importantly, how to write them.

In middle school I remember staying up to watch *The Tonight Show with Jay Leno*. At the time, Leno had just taken over Letterman in the ratings. Most people preferred Letterman's interviewing style. Leno knew it, so he played to his strength: telling jokes.

Leno's extended monologue was a masterclass in comedy—and copywriting. The jokes were contextual, concise, and made sense to the listener. They were basically headlines with a surprise ending. The whole art and craft of this type of writing fascinated me. In my opinion, the monologue was always the best part of late-night TV.

Six years ago, I came across a website called comedywire.com where anyone could post monologue-type jokes or responses to the day's news headlines. One service they offered was hourly training from former late night writers.

Gabe Abelson was the head monologue writer for David Letterman from 1997–2001. His rate was $50 an hour and, to this day, it remains the best money I've spent.

We corresponded by email and I sent him a few pages of jokes. He would mark up my Word doc and then we'd hop on the phone to discuss the edits. One of the things I liked about Gabe was he was very fatherly. Sometimes he'd go, "Josh, Josh, Josh," after he read one of my jokes that didn't hit the mark. But he was also encouraging in those few instances where I *did* hit the mark.

Here are a few jokes I sent to Gabe that didn't work or needed reworking. I included these for a peak-behind-the-curtain, if you will.

There are new reports that Viagra could help with altitude sickness. Ladies, be careful the next time a man asks if you want to climb Everest.
Too much to think about here. The logic is a bit thin. Viagra helps with altitude sickness. What would that have to do with a man wanting a woman to climb Everest? Because it's high? Not enough. He could still take Viagra and have sex with her at sea level. Just

climbing Everest won't want to make her have sex with a man any more than if she didn't climb it. This joke would only work if "heights" made a woman hornier. Viagra doesn't even make men horny. It's simply a physical "aid," so to speak.

A new study says that you can live longer by eating certain types of cheese. Participants were not only grated, they were shredded, sliced, and added to hamburgers for a dollar extra.
Doesn't work. Makes no sense. Right now, the most important thing for you, Josh, is to make sure your logic is airtight. And stay away from puns at all costs. Wordplay CAN work if it's more than just linguistics, if there's a strong visual associated with it, or if it's a play on an expression. But pure puns or double entendres will NOT work in monologue.

Nike will release self-lacing shoes for $700. In an attempt to get Americans more active, Nike announced its new slogan: Just let us do it.
MORE active? Isn't it the other way around? And if that's the point you're obfuscating it. I can see Jay Leno tackling this story because he loves to talk about

how fat and lazy Americans are. We'll re-tool this joke together. It's a great premise; you just need to flip the punchline. Also, don't use future words like "will release" when you can fudge it a bit and say "Nike is releasing … " And there's no apostrophe in "its" unless it's the contraction of "it is," in which case it's "it's." That kind of grammatical error can cost you a job. And put the slogan in quotation marks. This shit is important.

Maybe set up your premise like this:

Here's how lazy Americans are becoming: Nike is releasing self-lacing shoes for $700. In fact, Nike announced its new slogan: "Just let us do it."

A Domino's in New Zealand made history by having a drone deliver pizza. They're calling the delivery a landmark moment. Not because of the drone—because they actually remembered the cheesy bread.

C'mon, a drone delivering pizza? You can do better than this, Josh! Where's the drone in the punchline? Again, your associations need to be much stronger. Your twists need to be stronger.

For example:

A Domino's in New Zealand made history by having

a drone deliver pizza. They're calling the delivery a "tremendous success." Apparently the pizza drone took out the #3 leader of ISIS.

Not the best joke, but do you see the difference? I've tied in a completely different association (ISIS) in an unexpected way. You need to do more of that.

Experts are saying Trump's presidency could negatively impact the athletic shoe industry. Unaffected though will be those who flip-flop.
Pure pun. Nope. Also, the setup raises more questions than it answers, and that's the kiss of death for a joke. We want to know what that first statement MEANS. Again, it goes back to people understanding the setup.

It's now common for Millennials to date six people at once. The generation tends to lean towards the left but apparently has no problem swiping right.
Smart joke, but needs to be reworded.

This sampling came from 35 jokes I had sent him. According to Gabe, only 12 of the 35 worked. If you're a baseball player, that's about a .340 batting average. Not bad, but it could be better.

Working with Gabe and a few other late-night writers really helped me tighten things up for future headline and social media writing. I found how to say more with less and write in a cleaner, simpler way.

Here's a quick breakdown:

Be concise. 99.9% of the time, a monologue joke—or in our case, the subject lines—will be under two lines and no more than two sentences. Why? The audience has to be able to understand the setup, so they can appreciate the punchline, or with copy, the benefit. As Gabe would say, make sure it's "airtight."

Read a lot. Monologue writers have to capitalize on today's news. Chris Rock is known for reading multiple newspapers every morning, and just about every monologue writer does the same thing. The joke, and the news it's based on, has to be topical. For a copywriter, this might be reading things like *Adweek* or *Adage*. For me, it's Twitter, which has lowered my quality of life, but has kept me decently informed.

Write a lot. Like I mentioned in the chapter "The Good Goo," joke writing is a volume game. Monologue writers will write anywhere from 20—40 jokes in a day hoping one or two will make it to air.

Write what people know. Starbucks, the President, the Kardashians, Walmart, and more Kardashians. You have to start off with something everyone is familiar with. Find ways to relate that thing back to the product or service you're trying to sell to your copy.

Make the joke "fall off." A monologue joke only works when the final or second-to-last word takes the audience in a different direction; it's a last-second zig when everyone else thinks you will zag. Much like a monologue joke, copywriting is all about surprising people and showing them the truth that's right in front of their noses.

Against my better judgment, here are some of my best monologue jokes. I probably wrote a few thousand of them. Maybe 15—20 were okay. Guess you had to be there.

A woman burnt from Starbucks coffee was awarded $100,000. Even crazier? The check she was given had her name spelled correctly.

The new Baywatch movie comes out this weekend. It stars The Rock, Zac Efron, and a small cameo from shirts.

A Danish brewery launched a new beer made with urine. Even worse? They're being sued for stealing the recipe from PBR.

New studies show Millennials are going bald from stress. Yeah, now when a young person takes a selfie, it's just to get a better look at their hairline.

A porn star had her foot bitten by a shark in an underwater shoot. Even crazier? The shark wasn't even dressed up as a pizza delivery guy.

PRO
WRESTLING

In 2009, while still doing stand-up off and on, curiosity got the best of me and I decided I wanted to see what it took to become a pro wrestler. At the time (and of this writing) I was 5' 5" and 130 pounds. Not exactly a pillar of intimidation.

I had researched pro wrestling schools around the country because yes, these actually exist. And I'd spend hours reading what they were all about. Finally, I saw an ad on Craigslist for Firestorm Pro Wrestling (out of Cleveland), and they were holding open tryouts.

Before we go any further, it's probably worth mentioning why a story about wrestling would be in a copywriting book. The word I keep coming back to is: curiosity. Hollywood producer Brian Grazer says, "Curiosity is itself a form of power, and also a form of courage."

Curiosity is the copywriter's secret weapon and what separates them from account folks. It's the willingness to find the obvious truths about a product that is right in front of our eyes but only you can see. Looking into pro wrestling was just another step in my education of curiosity. I'll expand more on this later.

In the pro wrestling world, small independent promotions are scattered throughout the country, holding shows in high school gyms and small music venues. These smaller promotions act as the "minor leagues" of pro wrestling. Firestorm was no different.

The open tryout was at a place called the Phantasy Theater in nearby Lakewood, Ohio. The Phantasy was usually reserved for metal and punk bands, but on that day, it was reserved for wannabe wrestlers. Since it was February in Cleveland, sunshine was nowhere to be found.

When I walked into the Phantasy, I noticed I didn't feel much warmer. I found out later that in order to get a deal on the space, the wrestling promotion agreed to forgo heat and running water. It was a real Mickey Rourke/Randy "The Ram" Robinson vibe from *The Wrestler*.

As I approached the ring, there were 10–12 guys of all shapes and sizes. One guy was shorter than me but had a more muscular build like he had wrestled in high school or in college.

Another guy was built like a lumberjack. Probably close to 300 pounds with a big beard and a gut to match. This wasn't exactly WrestleMania.

Looking at the ring and all the guys in it was like looking at a creative brief. I thought, "How does this all fit together?" The wrestler in me was trying to figure it out. The copywriter in me, years later, does the same thing. And when a match or a copywriting project is about to begin, an empty ring and an empty page can be intimidating for different reasons.

When we finally gathered in the ring, the first thing the instructors asked us to do was "run the ropes." You know how you see pro wrestlers bounce off the ropes effortlessly before they get clotheslined or flipped in the air? Turns out it's not easy.

We took turns running the ropes for 60 seconds. I quickly found out that this type of workout was wrestling's version of gassers. Guys were winded, hands over their head or at their hips, and a few even threw up in a trash can nearby. Coming into it, I felt like I was in decent shape, but I was nowhere near what was required for wrestling.

Another "aha" moment was the feeling of when my back hit the ropes. On TV, the ropes look so soft and inviting. In reality, at least on the local level, they were made of steel cables wrapped in electrical tape.

Running the ropes is an art. There's a certain three-step dance you do as you run across the ring. At the last second, you have to turn your back to the ropes in order to bounce off. Not only do you have to bounce off, but the top rope has to land somewhere just beneath your shoulder blades to catapult you the right way. After doing this a few times, I could tell my back would be sore for days to come.

After running the ropes, the second thing we learned to do was bump. "Bumping" in the pro wrestling world is basically learning how to fall correctly. When a wrestler gets body slammed or takes a clothesline across the chest, they have to hit the mat with their back covering as much area as possible. This is so the shock of the fall is evenly dispersed throughout your body.

Learning to bump in wrestling is the equivalent to learning how to take feedback as a copywriter. It's learning how to fall—and get back up. Though sometimes feedback can be more painful than falling in a ring.

About three months into training, we had a practice where we focused exclusively on shoulder-tackle bumping.

With another wrestling student, I'd bounce off the ropes and lunge my right shoulder into his right shoulder.

These drills moved at a breakneck pace. You deliver a shoulder tackle-bump, then take a shoulder tackle-bump, then do it all over. You're up, you're down, and you're trying to keep the match moving. After the drill, I was exhausted, but I felt like I was getting the hang of this pro wrestling thing.

When I woke up the next morning, the room was spinning. Up to that point in my life, I had never experienced vertigo.

Apparently during the frenzy of taking bumps, my head hit the mat the wrong way at least a dozen times.

I went to a neurologist who told me what I already knew—I had a mild concussion. When I told him what caused it, he smiled and said, "My son plays college hockey, and I can't wait until he's done. He's gotten a couple of concussions, too. I would tell you the same thing I'd tell my son. If you have better—and safer—career options, quit wrestling."

My pro wrestling "career" (MAJOR air quotes) had come to an end. Actually, it was only 90 days and I never wrestled a match in front of an audience.

Unlike stand-up, Laugh Staff, or monologue jokes,

I'm not a copywriter, but ...

wrestling didn't help me refine or improve my writing. But it did reinforce the habits I needed to continue so that I could keep writing.

Running the ropes and bumping are fundamental to pro wrestling the same way reading and writing is to copywriting.

If a wrestler doesn't run the ropes consistently, they won't be in wrestling shape. And if a copywriter doesn't read consistently, they won't be in creative shape.

If a wrestler doesn't bump consistently, they risk injury. And if a copywriter doesn't write consistently, they risk injuring their writing voice.

And if we're being honest, I've always admired people who had relentlessly pursued perfecting the fundamentals.

Curiosity got me into the ring, and common sense got me out. If you can combine these two elements within your writing, you'll find yourself in the main event.

One of the instructors from that class started teaching again in 2020. I still kept in touch with him every now and then on Facebook. I didn't necessarily have regrets about not having a real match, but I always thought it would be cool to at least perform once—kind of like my dad did with stand-up.

The dreamer in me thought it would be interesting to learn the basics again at age 38 and get enough training to have at least one debut/farewell match at 40. Most copywriters are daydreamers, so this shouldn't surprise anyone. Again, curiosity got its claws in me.

I told my wife about the idea and she politely reminded me that anytime I have a health scare, I act like I'm dying. I knew if I did attempt to learn wrestling again, it wouldn't be "if" but "when" I would get another concussion (or worse). That concussion and resulting vertigo shook me to my core, and like The Red Hot Chili Peppers said in "Under the Bridge," "I don't ever wanna feel like I did that day."

Needless to say, I stayed retired.

SUMMARY

There's other copywriting books out there. In fact, I mentioned many of them throughout this book (and in the bibliography at the end). Since you're almost done reading this, I suggest you go read those. The more copywriters who tell their stories, and the more copywriters who read those stories, the better.

Here is a summary of the ideas we covered:

- Find your "good goo"—the time of day where you write and think clearly.
- As Seinfeld says, "Nobody writes all day." Not even copywriters.
- Make sure you're in a good location when you sit down to work.
- Keep slingin' big ideas, even in the face of criticism.
- Feedback is part of having skin in the game.
- You're not the only effective copywriter in the world. Or the only one with good ideas.
- Getting eyeballs on your work means it's worth reading. Don't fear the reaper.

- A healthy fear is, well, healthy if you're a copywriter.
- Amateurs have egos, pros to do, but can manage them.
- Abandoned buildings get you to think.
- Remember to shake the Etch A Sketch.
- The book is the buffalo. Use every part.
- Connect people and ideas. It will make you an invaluable copywriter.
- Don't let your ego get in the way of your success.
- When it comes to headlines, remember the safe, the stretch, and the really far out there.
- Subject lines, preheaders, and headlines will be there for you when the body copy doesn't come as readily. Rely on them.
- Body copy rolls downhill. It should reinforce the great decision the customer is about to make.
- If you don't find yourself saying "I wish I would've written that" once in a while, you're in the wrong room.
- It takes years and experience to write simply.
- Clients and creative directors love direct mail. You should too.

CONCLUSION

In *On Writing: A Memoir of the Craft*, Stephen King says, "John Grisham, of course, knows lawyers. What you know makes you unique in some other way."

King's remark goes back to Thomas Kemeny's quote from the beginning of this book:

"Everyone has some past knowledge or history that they bring to the table. Past jobs or hobbies that define you. Put that into your work and it won't feel like an ad and won't look like anyone else's."

The experiences of stand-up, Laugh Staff, monologue jokes, and pro wrestling make up my copywriting life experiences. You'll have your own experiences you come to the table with. One copywriter I worked with studied ballet in college, and another was a former sports reporter for a mid-market newspaper. That's the beautiful thing about copywriting: Late bloomers are welcomed. You might think you're getting into the game a little late, but really, you're stocking up on unique experiences, conversations, and learnings that will make you unlike any other copywriter.

If you're just starting out, straight out of ad school or college, you'll have experiences to draw on, too. Maybe during college you worked as a bartender or server. This is huge. You were talking to people consistently, representing a brand (whatever restaurant you were at) and getting a feel of how people talked in real life, not in a lecture hall. The same would be true if you were an ice cream scooper or barista.

Or perhaps during high school you worked as a landscaper, where you probably got a feel for design. You would mow, edge, mulch, and then take a step back to look at the finished product. If you saw something out of place, like a rogue blade of grass, you took care of it.

Hopefully as you read the experiences I shared, a central theme of curiosity—there's that word again—became apparent.

When the vice president at my internship told me I wasn't a great intern but that I was kind of funny, I got curious about learning stand-up.

When Cameron told me about the idea of comedians writing wedding toasts, I got curious about the potential business idea of humor writing.

When I watched Jay Leno do his monologues, I got

curious about who came up with his jokes and how they were written.

And when I researched pro wrestling schools, I got curious about how one goes about learning, and bouncing off of, the ropes.

Curiosity keeps the copywriter humble and dumb. "Dumb" isn't a bad thing, either. It's putting yourself in the position of the consumer, going back to the old Ogilvyism of:

"The consumer isn't a moron; she is your wife. You insult her intelligence if you assume that a mere slogan and a few vapid adjectives will persuade her to buy anything. She wants all the information you can give her."

I've been lucky enough to work with some really talented, curious, and down-to-earth copywriters. I think most of them would agree curiosity has helped them tackle tough briefs. And I think many of them feel lucky to be copywriters in general.

A couple years ago, I wrote a blog where I asked a collection of writers what they were most thankful for around the holidays; the article ran on musebycl. io the day before Thanksgiving. One of the responses that stuck out was from the godfather of copywriting himself, Luke Sullivan, author of *Hey Whipple, Squeeze*

This: The Classic Guide to Creating Great Ads. And let's be honest, this wouldn't be a true copywriting book without a Whipple reference.

Here's how Sullivan answered the question of, "What are you grateful for this holiday?"

"As a writer, I am thankful that I get to use my brain for a living and not my back. I am thankful I get to put my feet up on the burled mahogany of the agency's conference room desk, sitting in a nicely appointed meeting room at a hip renovated suite in the warehouse district. Not in a warehouse lifting boxes or operating a forklift, which is basically the kind of work most people in the world do for a living. Every day. Eight, 10, 12 hours a day."

Obviously there's nothing wrong with lifting boxes or driving forklifts, but I think we get his point. We play a kid's game for a king's ransom. Copywriting isn't really work, it's fun with purpose.

I always thought the character of Dexter Morgan, from Showtime's *Dexter,* represented the quirky ways of a copywriter.

In the show, Dexter is a blood spatter analyst for the Miami Metro Police Department. He doesn't hold the same authority or bravado as a detective, but his recognition of blood trajectory can make or break a case.

In the show, Dexter is constantly in his head problem solving. On the surface, he comes off as aloof and kind of dorky, but in reality, he's playing chess while everyone else is playing checkers.

Just like how blood spatter can make or break a case, a headline can make or break an ad. Like Dexter, copywriters live in their own heads. And also like Dexter, copywriters often can see blood on the wall, or words on the page, and begin to solve the puzzle. So, here's to the quiet moments when it's just you and your Word doc. And to the unquiet mind that makes you a copywriter.

Acknowledgments

A lifetime of great people helped make this book happen. No man is an island.

To Lauren, for marrying a grumpy, quirky copywriter and always being the voice of reason. I'd be in the gutter without you. Or Mayfield.

To Mom, I know, I know, I get my sense of humor from you. You're a wonderful mom and nana.

To Dad, for instilling in me a love of reading and learning. Now hit the steam room.

To Jay, for always looking out for me. And for my undying love for hair metal.

To Tina, for somehow living with the Womacks' sense of humor.

To Mikester, for being a little brother I can look up to.

To Max and Maddie, for the pleasure of watching you grow. Don't get too old to hang out with me!

To Denise and David, for being such amazing examples of marriage, friendship. And the cave.

To Jason, great minds think alike. And great minds will always visit McKay's.

To Anna, for bringing the New Yorker out of me at Barnes & Noble.

To my other family, the Sovas. Car's warmin' up.

To Luca and Dave, get a couple of these in ya ...

To Adam, Frank, and Mums. When we started this band, all we needed, needed was a laugh ...

To the late Belinda Wiggins, you were right, I wasn't a good intern.

To Jason Lawhead, for getting me onstage at Hilarities. That George Will elevator bit still makes me smile.

To Cameron, one day we will celebrate a Browns Super Bowl. And it will be miraculous.

To Brad, for your patience and guidance. Chirp, chirp.

To Eddie and Rebecca, for being awesome, intelligent writers to lean on for a project like this.

Bibliography

Boulton, Andrew and GilesEdwards. *Copywriting Is ... 30-or-so thoughts on thinking like a copywriter*. Harriman House, 2021.Catmull, Edwin and Amy Wallace. *Creativity, Inc.: Overcoming the Unseen Forces That Stand in the Way of True Inspiration*. Random House, 2014.

Ferriss, Tim. Jerry Seinfeld — A Comedy Legend's Systems, Routines, and Methods for Success (#485). *The Tim Ferriss Show*. Podcast audio. December 8, 2020. Jerry Seinfeld — A Comedy Legend's Systems, Routines, and Methods for Success (#485). https://tim.blog/2020/12/08/jerry-seinfeld/

Kemeny, Thomas. *Junior: Writing Your Way Ahead in Advertising*. powerHouse Books, 2019.

King, Stephen, *On Writing: A Memoir of the Craft*. Scribner, 2010.

Ogilvy, David. *Ogilvy on Advertising*. Vintage Books, 1983.

Pressfield, Steven. *The War of Art: Winning the Inner Creative Battles*. Rugged Land, 2002.

Pressfield, Steven. *Turning Pro: Tap Your Inner Power and Create Your Life's Work.* Black Irish Entertainment LLC, 2012.

Stulberg, Brad, Steve Magness, and Christopher Lane. *The Passion Paradox: A Guide to Going All In, Finding Success, and Discovering the Benefits of an Unbalanced Life.* Rodale Books, 2019.

Womack, Josh. "4 Life Lessons I Learned From My Short Stint as a Pro Wrestler". Entrepreneur. May 20, 2020. https://www.entrepreneur.com/article/348598

Womack, Josh. "5 ways you can get more comfortable taking criticism". Fast Company. February 10, 2020. https://www.fastcompany.com/90461922/4-ways-you-can-get-more-comfortable-taking-criticism

Womack, Josh. "What Writers Are Grateful for This Holiday." Muse by Clio. November 26, 2019. https://musebycl.io/musings/what-writers-are-grateful-holiday